AF364614

*revised and expanded edition*
©2022
Reine Nust

Red Admiral Press
*www.redadmiralpress.com*
Amsterdam, the Netherlands
9 8 7 6 5 4 3 2 1
978-90-833042-0-5

# THE ARCHICAT

**REINE NUST**

Sometimes, you might get that feeling that there's something
 you could learn from your cat.
But what could that be ?

The archicat explains.

# THE ARCHICAT

Archicature is no joke!

## The archicat explains ...

Yes, even cats!

Unfortunately there are still too many people that have a rather poor grasp of the principles of archicatural design ...

... I could point to the mice. Granted, mice have a certain level of understanding of what archicature is about...
It is clear, though, that their concept is hopelessly outdated, stuck in the forms of a former time ...
... a Roman arch in the 21st century? Come on, folks!

... but they have a misplaced fondness for the space in between rooms ...
We archicats call it "poché" space ...
... might have worked for Louis XIV, but not for modern man!

Honey, the landlady called again today!
Shut up! I'm trying to read the paper!!
Cut it out, Huey and Dewey!!

... it results in overcrowded and unhygenic housing conditions ...

The archicat continues his penetrating analysis of what's wrong
with present-day architecture.

# THE ARCHICAT

Archicature is no joke!

... we saw that many still live in deplorable housing conditions. It is clear: we need a new archicature! And it should be based on simple and self-evident principles.
1. sleeping
2. eating
3. looking out of the window
4. sleeping
... the four essential functions !

... but it seems that designers are stuck in furry baroque!

Fortunately there is a new generation of architects who are looking for change ...
There is Maus van der Rohe, a talented mouse ...
... a French raven, who calls himself Lecorbu ...
... we have the same taste in glasses!
... a Dutch architect, Rem Colehare, surprises with his striking designs...
... and from America we have Frank Kitty!

The entrance of the house surely is the part that deserves special attention. How is it, then, that so often designers can't get it right?

# THE ARCHICAT

Archicature is no joke!

The archicat investigates the **elements of architecture**.
First, let's take a look at the door ...

... but where's the **door** ?!
very well ...

... people **do** think of putting in a gate for the post to come in ...

... but the only one to find that useful is a **dog** ...

It is clear: here lies a task for the designer.
After many hours of patient research ..

they called it a **cat flap** !

oh, the ignomy !

they called it a **cat flap** !
oh, the ignomy !

A brilliant solution, it seems !
Sadly, as happens all too often, the marketing department runs away with it ..

Even the best minds in the profession will find that there are
limits to what design may accomplish.

# THE ARCHICAT

Archicature is no joke!

... and is there really no other way to open this thing than having to use one's **head** ?

Back to the **drawing table**?
... nobody said the life of an archicat would be easy ...

Maybe the old-fashioned method is still the best ..

After all, it's not **really** about going outside, is it ?

Ever felt the need for a house coach to help you really understand the quality of the spaces in your house? The archicat is there to help!

# THE ARCHICAT

Archicature is no joke!

So, we saw that for many it still seems hard to get what archicature is about ...

.. but there are others that possess a fine sense of archicature. That would be **cats** !

Cats have an innate sense of **symmetry**, as we can see for ourselves day after day ...

Plus, cats have this special appreciation for how **spaces** meet and interpenetrate ...

be aware ...
breathe ..
center ...

... a deep love for that complex and rich liminal space where inside and outside meet ...

Cats understand the quality of the **empty** uncluttered space. Minimalism ...

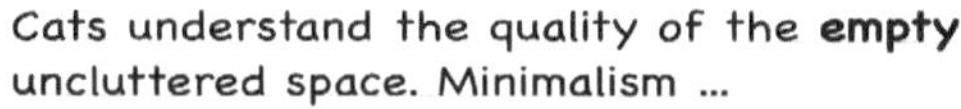

But, what is the **most** important characteristic of the spaces in archicature ?

Get it ?
it's **fun** !

What is your ideal place for working from home? The archicat
looks for the perfect workstation.

# THE ARCHICAT

Archicature is no joke!

We all know it: because of the corona virus we'd better work from **home** …
… hmmf … so we keep our-selves and others safe …
… can you hear me through this ?

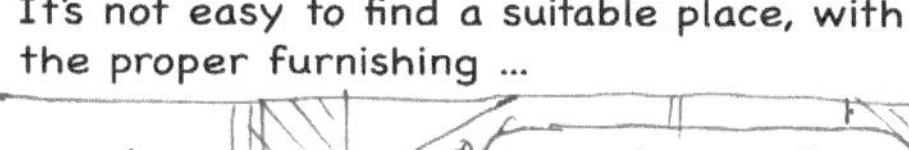

It's not easy to find a suitable place, with the proper furnishing …
… here … ?

… here … ?
… **mouse** is distracting …

… no room on this table …

Your workstation should be **comfortable**, and well-lit, with the proper **ventilation** and **heating**. It should be fitted with ergonomic furniture - nothing more **tiring** than a workplace that doesn't have the right **dimensions** …
… i think I found it …

… so that you can keep your **productivity** up, even in these **crazy** times …

The archicat has the answer ...

... but is it the right question?

# THE ARCHICAT

Archicature is no joke!

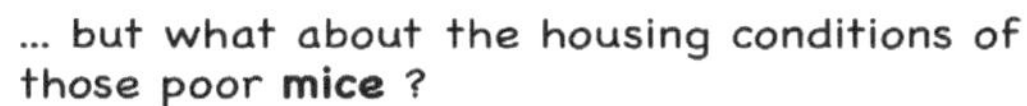
... but what about the housing conditions of those poor **mice** ?

zzzzzzzzzzzz
... the problem that we addressed a few weeks ago ...

huh ?!
what ?!
... errr ... what to do with these appalling conditions is still a hotly debated topic ...
Archicats have made many plans and proposals. But in the end there is only **one** remedy ...

**Sanitation** ! A ruthless and thorough **purge** ...
EVICTION

**Light** ! **Air** ! Well-regulated **traffic** !
But what shall we replace it with ? How can we provide **good**, yet **affordable**, housing ?

Location ... Orientation ... The proper distance between building blocks ...
... the **arrangement** is very important ...

Sadly, the mistaken nostalgia that the mice have for their old living quarters is **hard** to root out ...
POW

The archicat shows how you, too, can keep a safe distance.

# THE ARCHICAT

Archicature is no joke!

Just my luck! A conference of sardines ...
DISTANCE

Remember? The **packed** cars in public transport? That has changed a bit, hasn't it?

It's a **daily** job for us archicats to deal with measures ...
I, for instance, live on a grid with a unit of 5 millimetres ...
5

Now, everybody should keep a **distance**. But do we know how much that **is**?

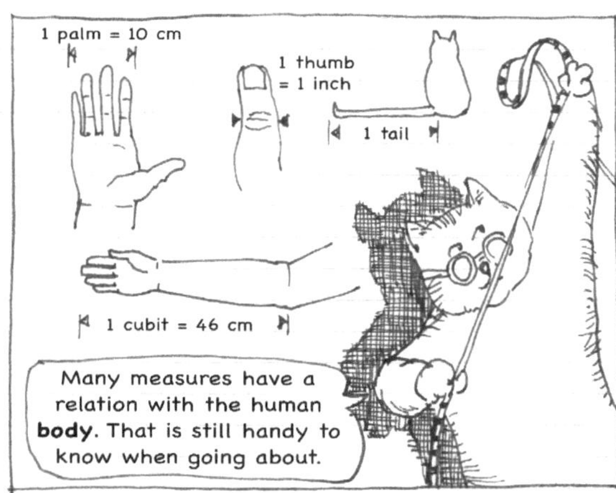

1 palm = 10 cm
1 thumb = 1 inch
1 tail
1 cubit = 46 cm

Many measures have a relation with the human **body**. That is still handy to know when going about.

Of course you can't go around walking like this ...
People **would** keep a distance though .. ...

A cat called Leonardo da Vinci put these **relations** in one succinct drawing ...

In Holland the concrete tiles of the **sidewalk** are usually 30 cm wide ...
30

It might be easier to count **tiles** ...
5 of these tiles equals 1.50 meter ...

And choosing the **right outfit** before going out could help !
What are you looking at ?
Are you looking at **me** ?!

Do you think that your interior lacks that *something*, that certain sparkle? The archicat gives you the options.

# THE ARCHICAT

Archicature is no joke!

... this space has decidedly too little going on ...

An important consideration, when designing interiors, is that cats like a certain **interest** in their environment ...

A mistake is adding too **much** interest. A labyrinth might be worthwhile for **mice**, but not for **cats** ...

Some architect has mentioned that a good plan is just about putting a **circle** in the right spot ...

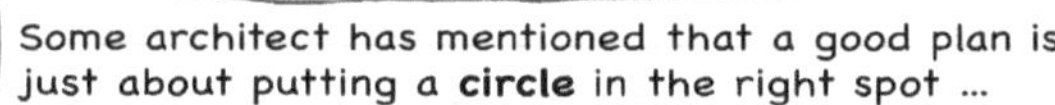

Better ...

... but this Aldolf Loos guy is **definitely** one of the cats !

There is also such a thing as doing too **much** ...

... and you get this irresistable urge ...

The archicat has a new client. But he struggles with this particular commission.

# THE ARCHICAT

Archicature is no joke!

I can't think of **anything** !

The archicat faces one of the **thorniest** challenges of the profession ...

... a house for your **nephew** ?
Why, **sure**, Mrs. Claypool !

A **dog** house ?  A **dog** house !

It may be out of the **comfort** zone ...
... but a great man has said ...
never say **no** !

The typology of the dog house hasn't **changed** significantly in the last 100 years ...

... time for a new concept ?
dog

... but it isn't **easy** ...!

So this is my client ...

... is there hope? Is there **some** idea ?

Oh, for some inspiration ...

Any archicat greets a new client with enthusiasm. But sometimes it can be very hard for each to understand the other properly.

# THE ARCHICAT

Archicature is no joke!

The archicat has a demanding new client. He is burning the midnight oil ...

Will we get **somewhere** today ?
Meetings are becoming very **frustrating** ...

A **bone** might be the perfect inspiration for the plan of your house ...
... I don't **understand** ...

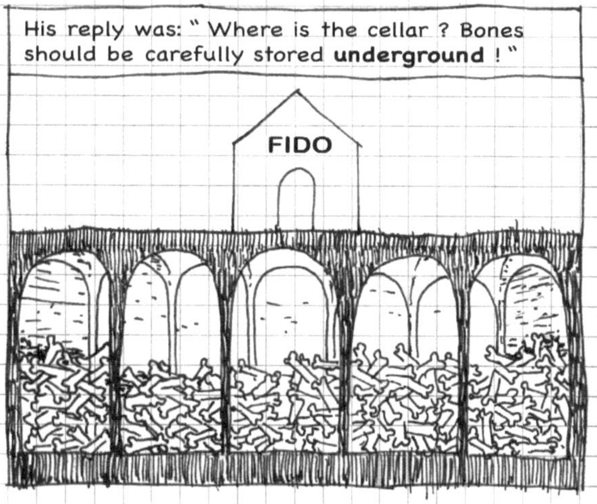

His reply was: " Where is the cellar ? Bones should be carefully stored **underground** ! "
FIDO

It is impossible to retain his **attention** at construction meetings ...
... so obviously the area for feeding should be next to ...

... especially around the time the **postman** does his rounds ...
sigh ...

Every design process has a learning curve. The archicat finds out
that this is a steep one.

# THE ARCHICAT

Archicature is no joke!

The **archicat** works diligently on his new project ...
Let's not forget the location of the **restroom** ...
... got to ask next time ...

Restroom ?!
Why, that **tree** over there of course !

Then, it turns out that he also needs a **gym** ...
... that is **twenty** times the size of the house ...

So I do my best to incorporate all this. I already spent **twice** the time that the budget allows ...

... and then he keeps **fetching** and returning my drawings and doesn't even **look** at them !

... and he insists on paying me with **old shoes, rubber balls** and **branches** !!!

It's always a special occasion when a building project is finished. The archicat thinks this will be the last dog house he'll ever deal with. Or is it ?

Archicature is no joke!

# THE ARCHICAT

Phew!
It's done! Today we'll visit the site for the **final** inspection of the house ...

Dogs have such **particular** wishes – I had **no** idea! Just think, it will be the first house I've designed that doesn't have a **scratching post** !
NO JOB NO MONEY

It's beautiful ...

... but I've decided to **sell** it ! It will remain in the family though. My **nephew** will buy it

... and by the way, he'll need an architect to make a few **alterations** ...

The archicat had some extra time lately. Maybe an occasion to watch the odd nature documentary and learn something ?

# THE ARCHICAT

Archicature is no joke!

I've been watching a lot of **nature documentaries** lately ...

... of course there's always an interest in species that are **endangered** ...
... and **rightly so** !
But why do they always have to be so damn **cute** !?
... it is ...
a **dormouse** !

Like **puffins**! Puffins are **overrated** ! Would-be **penguins** with their **two-tone suits** !  And those Picasso beaks !
hi !
It's **mating** season ! And all the puffins put on their best behaviour ...

Or take the **seals** !  They are really **dogs**, you know ... Oh, those watery droopy eyes - so cute, it makes me **sick** !
For the seal, the next few days are crucial . Will they be able to ...

But nobody shows any love for the **torrent midge** ... or McCarthy's **plant louse** ... or Gerlach's **cockroach** ....  And they are endangered **too** !
Oh man ! Why does everybody hate me !?

It's not about saving this or that cute animal. **All** animals, all living beings, are in need of each other . We all work **together** !  Whether you're **cute** or not ! It is about the **survival** of us all !
Yeah, I'm not cute either ! Are **archi-cats** endangered, I wonder ...?

**Summer night ...**

# THE ARCHICAT

Archicature is no joke!

Summer night ....
CLACKERADACK

... the archicat is asleep ....

... but what is that sound ?
KERA

It's a bicycle, riding on the bike path ..

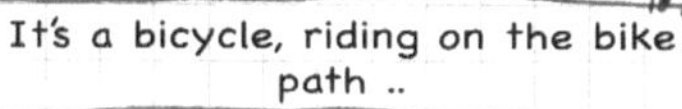

... the street tiles, over the dry weeks, have loosened ...

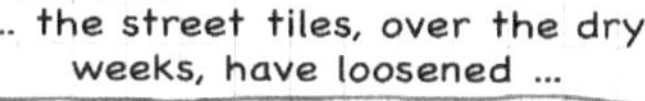

CLACK

... and rattle when the wheel hits them ...

... while up in the night sky ...

... a bat ...

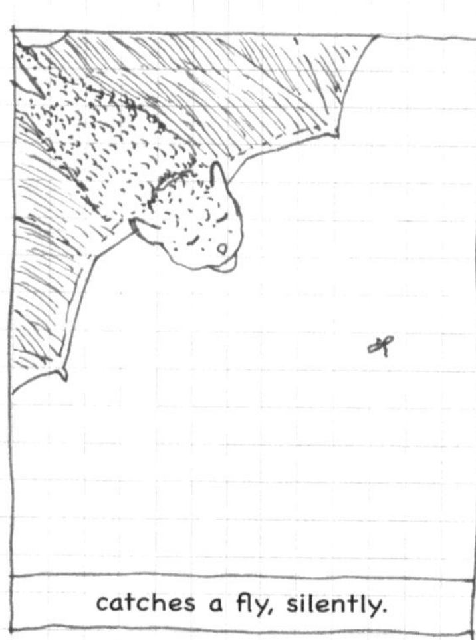

catches a fly, silently.

Dreams ...  a window into the subconscious ? A repository of suppressed wishes, or forgotten fears ?

# THE ARCHICAT

Archicature is no joke!

The archicat is asleep ....

... he has uneasy dreams ....
What is it, my dear man ?
Say, look here ! What is this supposed to be ?

Why, that's my **latest** design ...
So you admit that's yours, do you? **Scratching** posts, **catnip** garden, **litter** box room ... It's **ridiculous** !

But what can I do ? Catnip is **good** for you ...
I think you would do yourself a **favour** if you **quit** this job . It is an **insult** ...

... a **blatant** insult in the face of your clients ! Do you know who they are , at **all** ?!!
... but ... but ...

but ... but ...
bat ... bat ...

buzzzzz ...

buzzzzzzzz

Complete freedom in designing a house has its pitfalls.

# THE ARCHICAT

Archicature is no joke!

This is wonderful ....
... a **dream** commission !!
Complete freedom in designing
this villa, no **restraints** !!

It will have a dramatic **overhang** ! A sheer
glass box **jutting** out of the cliff side ...

An **infinity pool** of course ! Making a
**seamless** connection to the sea ...

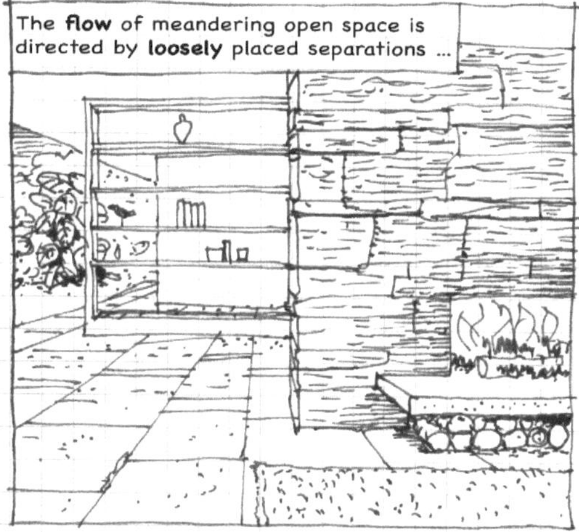

The **flow** of meandering open space is
directed by **loosely** placed separations ...

... a bathroom dedicated to luxurious **relaxing** ...
**dissolving** the boundary between inside and out ...
OK !!
**Enough**
already !!

Well, **great** ! But what
about **us** ?! Where are the
**walls** ? Where are **we** supposed to live ?!!

Some may think that there is something beyond archicature.
Or even without archicature. Really ...

# THE ARCHICAT

Archicature is ...
... a joke ?

Now, let's present a **different** view about architecture ...
Architecture without **archicats** !!

Take the termites, for instance . They make fantastic, naturally ventilated buildings that use the properties of heated air ...
It causes an **air circulation** that takes out the CO2 at night .
What's for dinner ?
Got a taste for a nice **suburban villa** ...

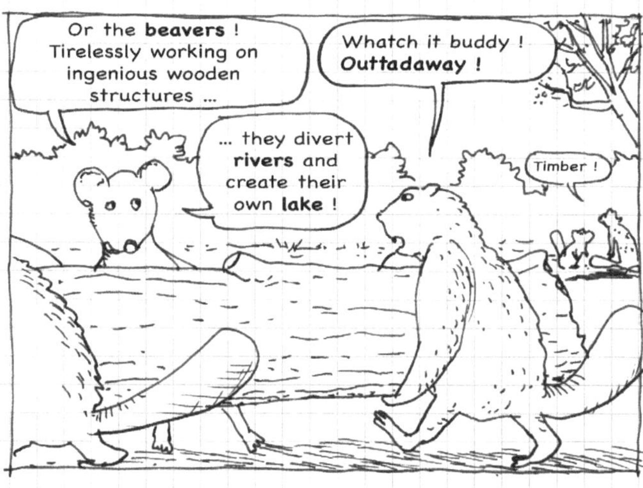

Or the **beavers** ! Tirelessly working on ingenious wooden structures ...
... they divert **rivers** and create their own **lake** !
Whatch it buddy ! **Outtadaway** !
Timber !

... the beauty, the exquisite **spontaneity**, with which **life** seeks and takes on its forms in an **accord** perfectly responsive to its **needs** ...
... **form** ever follows **function**, and this is the law ! And, as a great beaver once said: **Art** is the expression of an animal's **pleasure** in **labour** !
Hmmm, this is so **interesting** !

And here is the **architect** amongst the birds : the **bower bird** ! He makes his beautiful structure, only ...
.. to find a suitable **mate** !
What did **you** think ? You want to get the **chicks** in !
Architecture is all about **sex** !

... and what about **mice !?** What do they do ?
... euh ... we make our place in **walls** ...

... and **who** is the one making the walls, may I ask ?
... errrr ....

You can be hit by a ton of bricks if you're not careful around a building site. Or by an airplane. Or a virus. The archicat explains.

# THE ARCHICAT

Want to come outside ?
I'm not going anywhere !

Did you know there's a chance of one ...

... in 20.000 that an air-plane hits a house ?

Now, that's not just plain dumb bad luck ! Your decisions matter ...
Tea anyone ?
Two lumps, please.

For instance, building your house on a runway might be a bad idea ...
Your choices influence that chance, for the good or the bad.
... but I do love that the tax-free shop is around the corner !

The same with catching a contagious virus ! Your choices can help you avoid catching a really nasty disease. Or the chance of you infecting others ...

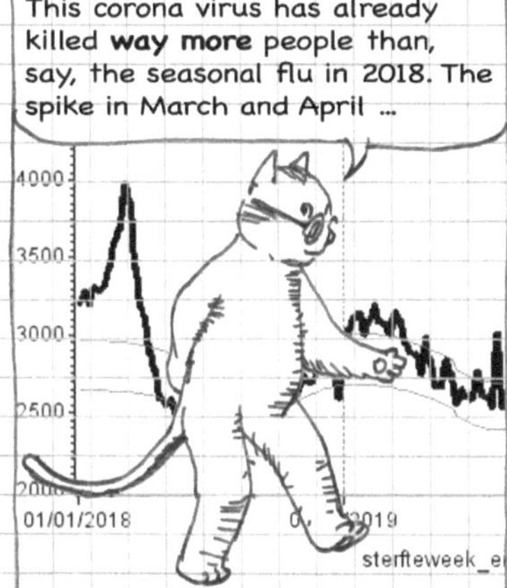

This corona virus has already killed way more people than, say, the seasonal flu in 2018. The spike in March and April ...
4000
3500
3000
2500
2000
01/01/2018
01/01/2019
sterfteweek_e

... was contained. But only because everybody used a mask ...
01/01/2020
01/...
atum

... was distancing, and washed their hands. Each of these is not 100% perfect by itself, but they all add up. You can minimise the chance !
That cat is too close for comfort ...
Better stay inside, love !

graph from Dutch National Institute for Public Health and the Environment, october 1, 2020

You might think that you know everything about the great
achievements of the old Egyptians. But the archicat doesn't
rest. On his trip to Giza he is duly impressed by the
achievements of his predecessors.

# THE ARCHICAT

How do I look ?
Mweh ...

The **pyramids** !  Foundation of architecture ! Great artificial mountains made with incredible **accuracy**. This one, the Pyramid of Khufu, built 4580 years ago ...

... is based on a triangle that contains the **golden ratio** ! The tallest structure for more than 3800 years, built in less than 20 years - faster than many infrastructural works **today**. And it still stands !

I like the Egyptians. They built **solidly.** And they had a quite sensible love of **cats**. The cat goddess **Bastet** was celebrated in her temple in the town of **Bubastis**, with great drunken **parties**.

But **architects** had a great status as well. They got their own grave monuments and were revered as **gods** !

Like **Imhotep** or Hemi-unu, who did this pyramid. They made calculations and drawings. On **graph paper** !

Makes one feel somewhat like a **mouse**, being at the feet of these **giants** ...

And here is the **Sphynx** ! Enigmatic ... one of the biggest sculptures in the world ... and **nobody** knows who or what it represents ...

... its face may even have been recarved ! So, I proposed a **reconstruction** ...

We know that our archicat is not just any architect. Or just any cat. He's also a cartoon character ! So, of course, he is able to go back in time and visit the ancient city of Bubastis, where cats are considered quite special.

# THE ARCHICAT

"archikitty" ?

Here I am, in Egypt on a sunny morning **2500 years** ago, on my way to the great temple in **Bubastis** dedicated to **Bastet**, the **cat godess** !

A pleasant boat ride ... The temple is surrounded by water you see .

It's a feast day today ! From all over Egypt, hundreds of thousands of people gather, to celebrate ...

... and sing and dance, and drink wine. All in honour of **cats** ! We are thought to be the incarnation of **Bastet** ...

These people are so **friendly** !

They must marvel at seeing a **sacred animal** like me ...

I do wonder what they are saying **exactly** ...

Fortunately I thought of bringing my language guide, " How and What in **Ancient Egyptian** " !

" Here kitty kitty " ?!?

The archicat comes home, and he allows us a rare view of all the comforts of his apartment.

# THE ARCHICAT

Ahh, how nice to come back **home** ! Let me give you a **tour** of my house ...

My **favourite** spot ! By the window, looking out ...

... and right next to my **rich** collection of dirty pictures ... of **buildings** of course !

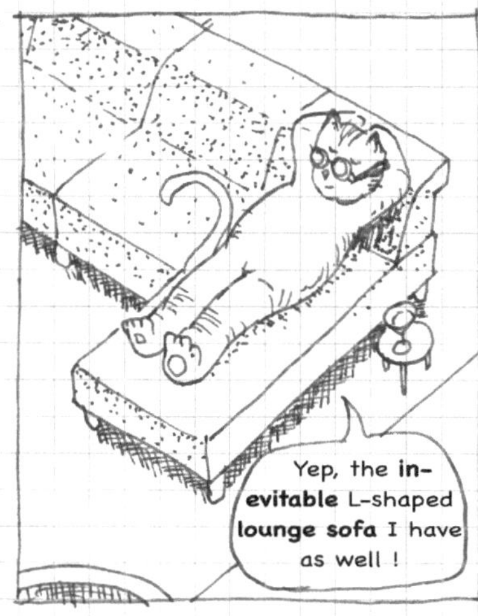

Yep, the **inevitable** L-shaped **lounge sofa** I have as well !

I designed the table **myself** ... A nice ...

... **conversation** piece ! And conveniently close to the **kitchen** !

The bathroom ... The **less** said, the **better** ...

... I **am** very pleased with my **bed** though !

But why is it that I always end up **here**, irresistibly drawn to the ol' **cardboard box** ... ?

**An Archicat's Advent:**
**Autumn is almost over ...**

# THE ARCHICAT

.. too early ...
ho ho ho ?

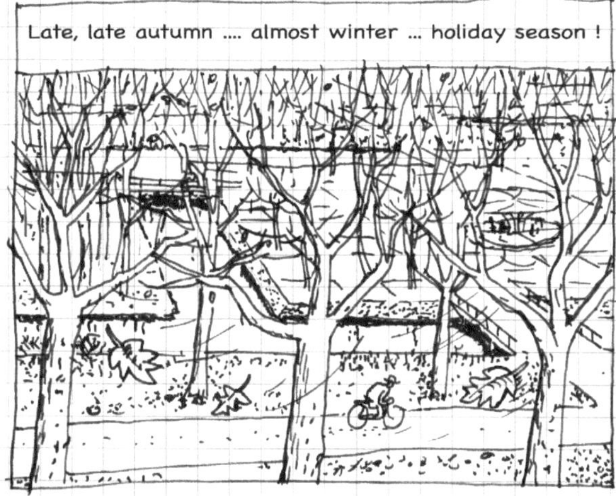

Late, late autumn .... almost winter ... holiday season !

Fitness workout is still going on in the park ...
Upside down !
Inside out !

That same group of guys in their down coats are still chatting and smoking on the bench ...

It becomes difficult to tell what it is underneath all those layers of coats and mufflers ...

Holiday cheer at the Albert Hamster, the local supermarket ...
... djingle bells
... djingle bells ...
   djingle ...
GOOD

... and it's already night at 4:30 ...
... and it's not even December yet !

An Archicat's Advent:
Oh, those days before Christmas can be misty...
Who could be out on a day like that?

# THE ARCHICAT

.. anyone there ?

Another misty day ...

Really, it hasn't let up for days now ! No wonder nobody is out ...
ho ho ho

o ho
ho ho ho

I can't believe it !
ho ho
ho ho ho

Christmas mice !
ho ho ho !
ho ho ho
ho ho ho !
ho ho ho !
ho ho

I bet you, too, are glad to learn about these handy design suggestions for Christmas!

# THE ARCHICAT

Where are you going ?
Out carolling !

Every year we meet with the same recurrent problems in our houses and apartments ...
In the holiday season it is no different !
As an archicat I look for solutions ...

On, Cupid ! On, Donner and ... hrmpf ! Oh, hang it !

Stuck in the ventilation duct again !

With no chimneys in apartment blocks, the solution here is a reverse laundry chute – a Yule launch !
Yipeeee !!!

Traditional homes have their own pitfalls – the roof is an unstable landing ground ...
Whoops !

This is where the flat roofs of our modern architecture can shine ...
S

Carolling mice ! So charming, so cute ! But in the case of a high rise apartment block ...
Hark the herald angels sing ...

... I can hardly hear a thing ! What can be done about this ?
Fortunately there is a solution ! I have ...
... a rather nice singing voice !
squeak !
squeak !

I wish yeaauww aay meeeaawwy
Christ meaaauwz !!
Oh please !!

Everyone likes to make lists at the end of the year, you know, the ups and the downs . The archicat has his own particular list.

# THE ARCHICAT

I couldn't wait till this year was **over** !  Finally, it's **2021** !

What a year it has been ...

The lines for the **cat food** ...
Hamsters left only two cans ... and they're not even **cats** !
Lekker !

Sure, enough work to do, but what **kind** of work ...
**Another** extension ?
A dog needs a **workplace** too !

... and not a **beaver** to be found to **build** it ...
Sorry buddy !  **Everybody** wants a lodge now !

... and that was not the **worst** ...

... it was all these illegal **mouse** parties !
Who let the dogs out !!
Nah ... I just **love** these **cat** kibbles !
Piece of **cheese** ?

Have you ever thought about this? What would the history of
architecture have been if humans hadn't lost the protection of
their comfortable hairy layer?

In this episode, you might recognise references to Laugier,
Khufu, Piranesi, the Burj Khalifa, and a project for a 170 km
long building in Saudi Arabia called "The Line".

THE ARCHICAT

Itchy fur ?

The archicat talks about something he sees with a lot of his clients.

No fur !

In fact, an astounding amount of creatures on this planet go about with a shocking lack of fur ! Where lies the origin for this ?

It's an old story ... A long time ago, having an **apple** in a garden ...

But... you have no fur !
Huh ?

An **awful** truth was discovered: they were **naked** !

Any ideas ?

What to do ? It was clear they needed some kind of **shelter** ...

You call that primitive hut a house ?!

Since then, there has been a never-ending attempt to make the **perfect** building .

Nice shape ... if it but only were bigger ...

Are you sure you used the right dimensions ?

Buildings got bigger and bigger. And higher and higher ...

Oh well, we were the tallest for 4000 years ...

... and longer and longer ...

There goes the neighbourhood !

... and all because of **no fur !**

As above so below, they say. The archicat has a healthy respect for the wonders of the golden ratio. You know of course that this ratio is used to hold each part of a building together, inside as well as outside. And that the proportions of a design like that reflect and embrace the cosmic order. The archicat finds out for himself.

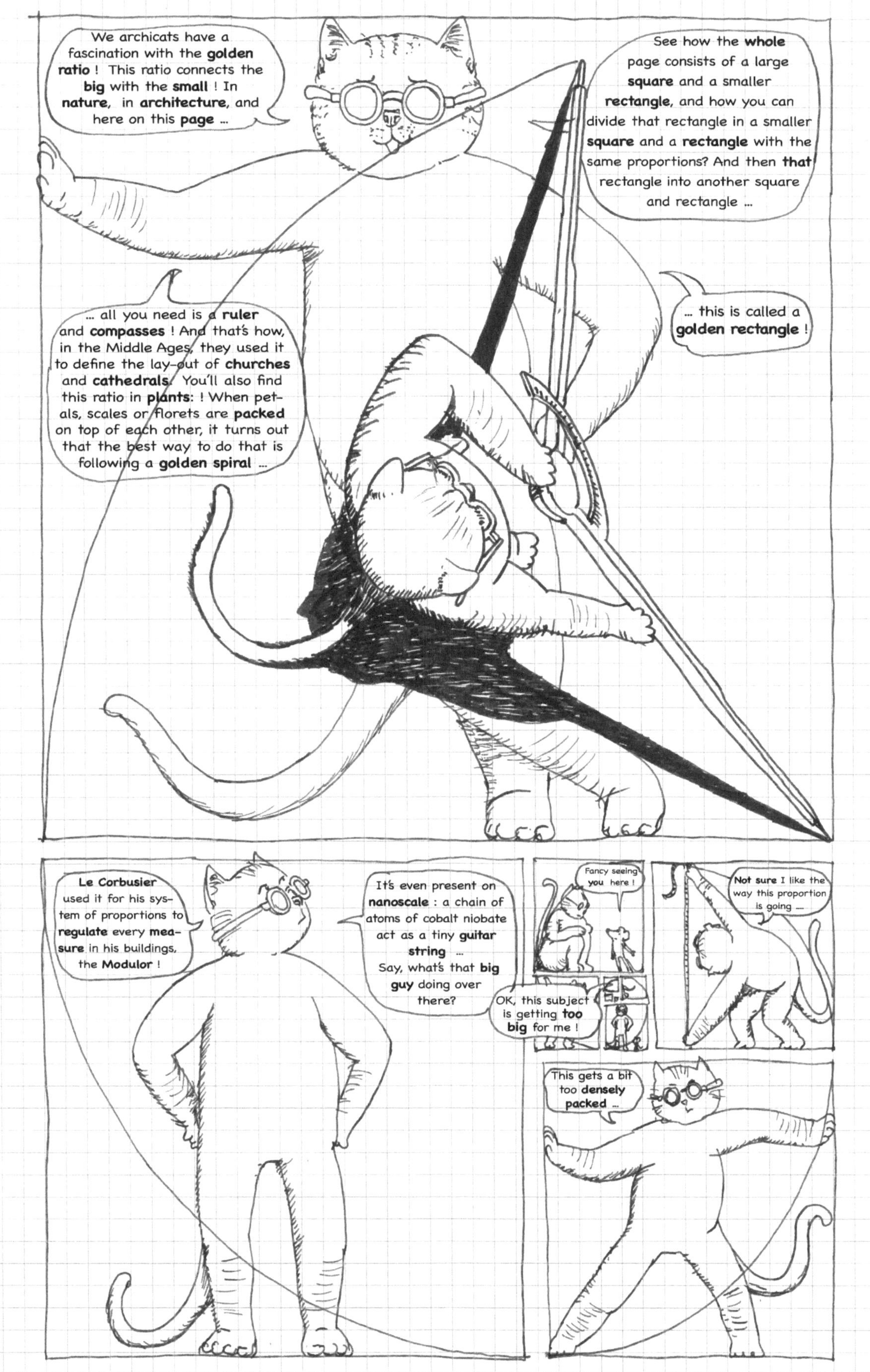

We archicats have a fascination with the **golden ratio** ! This ratio connects the **big** with the **small** ! In **nature**, in **architecture**, and here on this **page** ...
See how the **whole** page consists of a large **square** and a smaller **rectangle**, and how you can divide that rectangle in a smaller **square** and a **rectangle** with the same proportions? And then **that** rectangle into another square and rectangle ...
... this is called a **golden rectangle** !
... all you need is a **ruler** and **compasses** ! And that's how, in the Middle Ages, they used it to define the lay-out of **churches** and **cathedrals**. You'll also find this ratio in **plants**: ! When petals, scales or florets are **packed** on top of each other, it turns out that the best way to do that is following a **golden spiral** ...
**Le Corbusier** used it for his system of proportions to **regulate** every measure in his buildings, the **Modulor** !
It's even present on **nanoscale** : a chain of atoms of cobalt niobate act as a tiny **guitar string** ...
Say, what's that **big guy** doing over there?
Fancy seeing you here !
OK, this subject is getting **too big** for me !
**Not sure** I like the way this proportion is going —
This gets a bit too **densely** packed ...

# Now it's your turn!

Let's see what *you* have learned from the explanations of the archicat. He will set *you* a commission now, and on the graph paper opposite you can do your own design!

Can you show me the most efficient lay-out
for the placement of the cat box in relation to the
food bowls, the soft pillow, and the television
room ? Use only a pencil, and don't worry if you
make a mistake !

# OK, first one down !

**But you're not done yet ...**

That wasn't so easy, was it ?!  Well, we can't all be archicats in one day.
Let's see how you do with the design of a house with **walls** ! Take into account that a mouse family can have up to 13.000 little mice in a year ....

# Almost there !

You didn't think archicature was easy, or did you ?

That's right ! A house with **no walls** is the solution !   Well, from here on, you're on your own.  You can use this last piece of graph paper for your own ideas ... or maybe another **archicat episode** !